50 Sweet Spanish Recipes for Home

By: Kelly Johnson

Table of Contents

- Churros with Chocolate Sauce
- Tarta de Santiago (Almond Cake)
- Flan de Huevo (Spanish Custard)
- Turron de Jijona (Soft Almond Nougat)
- Crema Catalana (Spanish Crème Brûlée)
- Polvorones (Spanish Shortbread Cookies)
- Leche Frita (Fried Milk Custard)
- Rosquillas (Spanish Doughnuts)
- Pestiños (Honey Fritters)
- Torrijas (Spanish French Toast)
- Tarta de Queso (Spanish Cheesecake)
- Mantecados (Spanish Christmas Cookies)
- Alfajores (Spanish Sandwich Cookies)
- Bunuelos de Viento (Spanish Wind Fritters)
- Natillas (Spanish Custard)
- Magdalenas (Spanish Lemon Muffins)
- Pastissets (Spanish Pastry Cookies)
- Miguelitos (Puff Pastry Desserts)
- Tocino de Cielo (Spanish Egg Yolk Flan)
- Galletas Maria (Spanish Maria Biscuits)
- Empanada Gallega (Galician Meat Pie)
- Ensaïmada (Spanish Sweet Pastry)
- Polvorones de Almendra (Almond Powder Cookies)
- Cabello de Ángel (Angel Hair Pastry)
- Pudin de Pan (Spanish Bread Pudding)
- Bizcocho de Chocolate (Spanish Chocolate Cake)
- Tortas de Aceite (Spanish Olive Oil Biscuits)
- Crema de Calabaza (Spanish Pumpkin Cream)
- Torta de Manzana (Spanish Apple Cake)
- Alfajor de Medina Sidonia (Spanish Almond Cookie)
- Yemas de Santa Teresa (Spanish Egg Yolk Confections)
- Arroz con Leche (Spanish Rice Pudding)
- Tarta de Tres Leches (Spanish Three Milk Cake)
- Granizado de Limón (Spanish Lemon Granita)
- Mantecadas de Astorga (Spanish Sponge Cakes)

- Pionono (Spanish Rolled Sponge Cake)
- Buñuelos de Calabaza (Spanish Pumpkin Fritters)
- Torrijas de Vino (Wine-Soaked Spanish French Toast)
- Sobaos Pasiegos (Spanish Butter Cakes)
- Tarta de Chocolate y Almendras (Chocolate Almond Tart)
- Goxua (Basque Custard Dessert)
- Brazo de Gitano (Spanish Swiss Roll)
- Piñonate (Spanish Pine Nut Confection)
- Leche Merengada (Spanish Meringue Milk)
- Coca de Sant Joan (Spanish Midsummer Cake)
- Pan de Higos (Spanish Fig Bread)
- Cuajada (Spanish Curd Cheese Dessert)
- Almendrados (Spanish Almond Cookies)
- Suspiros de Monja (Spanish Nun's Sighs)
- Sopa de Fresas (Spanish Strawberry Soup)

Churros with Chocolate Sauce

Ingredients:

For the Churros:

- 1 cup water
- 2 tablespoons granulated sugar
- 1/2 teaspoon salt
- 2 tablespoons vegetable oil
- 1 cup all-purpose flour
- Vegetable oil, for frying

For the Chocolate Sauce:

- 4 oz (113g) dark chocolate, chopped
- 1/2 cup heavy cream
- 2 tablespoons granulated sugar
- 1/2 teaspoon vanilla extract

Instructions:

1. In a saucepan, combine the water, sugar, salt, and vegetable oil. Bring to a boil over medium heat.
2. Remove the saucepan from the heat and stir in the flour until it forms a smooth dough.
3. Heat vegetable oil in a deep fryer or a heavy-bottomed pot to 375°F (190°C).
4. Spoon the churro dough into a piping bag fitted with a large star tip.
5. Carefully pipe strips of dough into the hot oil, using scissors to cut them to your desired length. Fry the churros until golden brown, about 2-3 minutes per side. Transfer to a paper towel-lined plate to drain excess oil.
6. In a small saucepan, heat the heavy cream until it just begins to simmer.
7. Place the chopped dark chocolate in a heatproof bowl. Pour the hot cream over the chocolate and let it sit for 1-2 minutes.
8. Stir the chocolate mixture until smooth and glossy. Stir in the sugar and vanilla extract until well combined.

9. Serve the churros warm with the chocolate sauce for dipping.
10. Enjoy your homemade churros with chocolate sauce as a delightful dessert or snack!

These churros are crispy on the outside, soft and fluffy on the inside, and perfectly complemented by the rich and creamy chocolate sauce. They're sure to be a hit with family and friends!

Tarta de Santiago (Almond Cake)

Ingredients:

- 1 1/2 cups blanched almonds
- 1 cup granulated sugar
- 4 large eggs
- Zest of 1 lemon
- Zest of 1 orange
- 1 teaspoon almond extract (optional)
- Confectioners' sugar, for dusting

Instructions:

1. Preheat your oven to 350°F (175°C). Grease and flour a 9-inch round cake pan, then line the bottom with parchment paper.
2. In a food processor or blender, pulse the blanched almonds until finely ground. Be careful not to over-process them into almond butter.
3. In a large mixing bowl, beat the eggs and granulated sugar together until light and fluffy.
4. Stir in the ground almonds, lemon zest, orange zest, and almond extract (if using) until well combined. The batter will be thick and slightly sticky.
5. Pour the batter into the prepared cake pan and spread it evenly with a spatula.
6. Bake the cake in the preheated oven for 30-35 minutes, or until golden brown and a toothpick inserted into the center comes out clean.
7. Remove the cake from the oven and let it cool in the pan for 10 minutes.
8. Carefully invert the cake onto a wire rack to cool completely.
9. Once the cake has cooled, transfer it to a serving plate and dust the top with confectioners' sugar.
10. Serve slices of Tarta de Santiago on its own or with a dollop of whipped cream or a scoop of vanilla ice cream, if desired.
11. Enjoy the rich and nutty flavor of this traditional Spanish Almond Cake!

Tarta de Santiago is often adorned with the cross of Saint James, traditionally made by placing a stencil of the cross on top of the cake and dusting it with powdered sugar.

This simple yet elegant dessert is perfect for any occasion, whether you're celebrating a special holiday or simply craving a delicious slice of almond cake.

Flan de Huevo (Spanish Custard)

Ingredients:

For the Caramel:

- 1 cup granulated sugar
- 1/4 cup water

For the Custard:

- 4 large eggs
- 1 can (14 oz) sweetened condensed milk
- 1 can (12 oz) evaporated milk
- 1 teaspoon vanilla extract

Instructions:

1. Preheat your oven to 350°F (175°C). Place a large baking dish or roasting pan filled with about 1 inch of hot water in the oven to create a water bath.
2. To make the caramel, place the granulated sugar and water in a saucepan over medium heat. Stir until the sugar is dissolved.
3. Once the sugar has dissolved, stop stirring and let the mixture come to a boil. Continue cooking, swirling the pan occasionally, until the sugar caramelizes and turns a deep amber color, about 5-7 minutes.
4. Quickly pour the caramel into a 9-inch round cake pan, tilting the pan to coat the bottom evenly. Be careful as the caramel will be very hot. Set aside to cool and harden.
5. In a large mixing bowl, whisk together the eggs, sweetened condensed milk, evaporated milk, and vanilla extract until smooth and well combined.
6. Strain the custard mixture through a fine mesh sieve into a clean bowl to remove any lumps.
7. Pour the custard mixture over the cooled caramel in the cake pan.
8. Carefully transfer the cake pan to the preheated oven and place it in the water bath.

9. Bake the flan for 50-60 minutes, or until set around the edges but still slightly jiggly in the center.
10. Remove the flan from the oven and let it cool to room temperature.
11. Once cooled, cover the cake pan with plastic wrap and refrigerate the flan for at least 4 hours or overnight to chill and set completely.
12. To serve, run a knife around the edges of the cake pan to loosen the flan. Place a serving platter over the top of the pan and carefully invert the flan onto the platter. The caramel sauce will flow over the top of the flan.
13. Slice and serve the flan cold, drizzled with any remaining caramel sauce from the pan.

Enjoy the creamy and decadent texture of this classic Spanish custard dessert!

Turron de Jijona (Soft Almond Nougat)

Ingredients:

- 1 cup blanched almonds
- 1 cup honey
- 1 cup granulated sugar
- 1/4 cup water
- 1/4 teaspoon ground cinnamon (optional)

Instructions:

1. Begin by toasting the blanched almonds in a dry skillet over medium heat for 5-7 minutes, stirring frequently, until they are lightly golden and fragrant. Remove from heat and let them cool.
2. Once the almonds are cool, place them in a food processor and pulse until finely ground. You can also chop them finely by hand if you prefer a more rustic texture.
3. In a medium saucepan, combine the honey, granulated sugar, water, and ground cinnamon (if using). Stir the mixture over medium heat until the sugar is dissolved.
4. Insert a candy thermometer into the saucepan and cook the mixture, without stirring, until it reaches 280°F (138°C), also known as the hard crack stage.
5. Remove the saucepan from the heat and quickly stir in the ground almonds until they are evenly coated with the honey-sugar mixture.
6. Line a square or rectangular baking dish with parchment paper, leaving some overhang on the sides for easy removal later.
7. Pour the almond mixture into the prepared baking dish, using a spatula to smooth the top.
8. Allow the Turron de Jijona to cool completely at room temperature for several hours, or preferably overnight, until it has set and hardened.
9. Once set, use the parchment paper to lift the Turron out of the baking dish and transfer it to a cutting board.
10. Use a sharp knife to slice the Turron into small squares or rectangles.
11. Serve the Turron de Jijona as a sweet treat on its own, or alongside other traditional Spanish desserts.
12. Store any leftover Turron in an airtight container at room temperature for up to two weeks.

Enjoy this delightful Soft Almond Nougat as a traditional Spanish delicacy during holidays or special occasions, or simply as a delicious snack any time of year!

Crema Catalana (Spanish Crème Brûlée)

Ingredients:

- 4 cups (1 liter) whole milk
- Zest of 1 lemon
- Zest of 1 orange
- 1 cinnamon stick
- 6 large egg yolks
- 1 cup (200g) granulated sugar, divided
- 1/4 cup (30g) cornstarch
- 1 teaspoon vanilla extract
- Extra granulated sugar for caramelizing

Instructions:

1. In a saucepan, heat the milk, lemon zest, orange zest, and cinnamon stick over medium heat until it just begins to simmer. Remove from heat and let it steep for 10-15 minutes to infuse the flavors. Remove the cinnamon stick.
2. In a mixing bowl, whisk together the egg yolks, 3/4 cup of granulated sugar, cornstarch, and vanilla extract until smooth and pale.
3. Slowly pour the warm milk mixture into the egg yolk mixture, whisking constantly to prevent curdling.
4. Pour the mixture back into the saucepan and cook over medium heat, stirring constantly, until it thickens and coats the back of a spoon, about 5-7 minutes. Do not let it boil.
5. Once thickened, remove the saucepan from the heat and strain the mixture through a fine mesh sieve into a clean bowl to remove any lumps and the zest.
6. Divide the custard evenly among serving dishes or ramekins. Cover each dish with plastic wrap, pressing it directly onto the surface of the custard to prevent a skin from forming. Chill in the refrigerator for at least 2-3 hours, or until set.
7. Once the custard has chilled and set, sprinkle a thin, even layer of granulated sugar over the top of each serving.
8. Caramelize the sugar using a kitchen torch, moving the flame in a circular motion until the sugar melts and caramelizes to form a golden-brown crust. Alternatively, you can place the dishes under a preheated broiler for 1-2 minutes until the sugar caramelizes.

9. Let the Crema Catalana sit for a few minutes to allow the caramel to harden, then serve immediately.
10. Enjoy this delicious Spanish dessert with its creamy custard and crunchy caramelized sugar topping!

Crema Catalana is best served fresh, but you can prepare it in advance and caramelize the sugar just before serving for the best texture.

Polvorones (Spanish Shortbread Cookies)

Ingredients:

- 2 cups (250g) all-purpose flour
- 1 cup (120g) ground almonds or almond flour
- 3/4 cup (170g) unsalted butter, at room temperature
- 1/2 cup (100g) granulated sugar
- 1/2 teaspoon ground cinnamon
- 1/4 teaspoon ground cloves
- Pinch of salt
- Confectioners' sugar, for dusting

Instructions:

1. Preheat your oven to 350°F (175°C) and line a baking sheet with parchment paper.
2. In a large mixing bowl, combine the flour, ground almonds, granulated sugar, cinnamon, cloves, and salt.
3. Add the room temperature butter to the dry ingredients and use your hands or a pastry cutter to mix until the dough comes together and forms a cohesive ball. The dough should be crumbly but hold together when pressed.
4. Divide the dough into small portions and shape them into round balls, about 1 inch in diameter. Place the balls on the prepared baking sheet, spacing them slightly apart.
5. Gently press down on each ball with the palm of your hand to flatten slightly and create a cookie shape.
6. Bake the cookies in the preheated oven for 12-15 minutes, or until the edges are just beginning to turn golden brown.
7. Remove the cookies from the oven and let them cool on the baking sheet for a few minutes before transferring them to a wire rack to cool completely.
8. Once the cookies are completely cool, dust them generously with confectioners' sugar.
9. Serve and enjoy these crumbly and buttery Polvorones with a cup of coffee or tea!
10. Store any leftover cookies in an airtight container at room temperature for up to one week.

These traditional Spanish shortbread cookies are perfect for holiday gatherings, afternoon tea, or any time you're craving a sweet and crumbly treat. Enjoy making and sharing them with family and friends!

Leche Frita (Fried Milk Custard)

Ingredients:

For the Custard:

- 4 cups whole milk
- 1 cinnamon stick
- Zest of 1 lemon
- Zest of 1 orange
- 1 cup granulated sugar
- 1/2 cup cornstarch
- 4 large egg yolks

For Frying and Coating:

- Vegetable oil, for frying
- 1 cup all-purpose flour
- 2 large eggs, beaten
- 1 cup fine breadcrumbs
- Vegetable oil, for frying
- Granulated sugar, for dusting
- Ground cinnamon, for dusting

Instructions:

1. In a saucepan, heat the milk, cinnamon stick, lemon zest, and orange zest over medium heat until it just begins to simmer. Remove from heat and let it steep for 10-15 minutes to infuse the flavors. Remove the cinnamon stick and zest.
2. In a mixing bowl, whisk together the granulated sugar, cornstarch, and egg yolks until smooth and creamy.
3. Gradually pour the warm milk mixture into the egg mixture, whisking constantly to prevent curdling.
4. Pour the mixture back into the saucepan and cook over medium heat, stirring constantly, until it thickens and coats the back of a spoon, about 5-7 minutes. Do not let it boil.

5. Once thickened, pour the custard into a shallow dish or baking pan and smooth the top with a spatula. Let it cool to room temperature, then cover with plastic wrap and refrigerate for at least 2-3 hours, or until set.
6. Once the custard has chilled and set, use a sharp knife to cut it into squares or rectangles.
7. Prepare three shallow dishes for breading: one with flour, one with beaten eggs, and one with breadcrumbs.
8. Dredge each custard square in flour, shaking off any excess. Then dip it into the beaten eggs, allowing any excess to drip off. Finally, coat it evenly in breadcrumbs, pressing gently to adhere.
9. Heat vegetable oil in a deep fryer or heavy-bottomed pot to 350°F (175°C). Fry the breaded custard squares in batches until golden brown and crispy, about 2-3 minutes per side.
10. Remove the fried custard squares from the oil using a slotted spoon and transfer them to a paper towel-lined plate to drain excess oil.
11. While still warm, dust the fried custard squares generously with granulated sugar and ground cinnamon.
12. Serve the Leche Frita immediately as a delicious and indulgent dessert!

Leche Frita is best enjoyed warm and crispy, with its creamy custard filling melting in your mouth. It's a delightful treat that's sure to impress your family and friends!

Rosquillas (Spanish Doughnuts)

Ingredients:

For the Doughnuts:

- 2 cups (250g) all-purpose flour
- 1/2 cup (100g) granulated sugar
- 2 teaspoons baking powder
- Pinch of salt
- Zest of 1 lemon
- 2 large eggs
- 1/4 cup (60ml) milk
- 1/4 cup (60ml) olive oil or vegetable oil
- Vegetable oil, for frying

For the Glaze:

- 1 cup (120g) confectioners' sugar
- 2-3 tablespoons water
- 1/2 teaspoon vanilla extract

Instructions:

1. In a large mixing bowl, whisk together the flour, granulated sugar, baking powder, salt, and lemon zest.
2. In a separate bowl, beat the eggs lightly, then add the milk and olive oil. Whisk until well combined.
3. Pour the wet ingredients into the dry ingredients and mix until a soft dough forms. If the dough is too dry, you can add a little more milk, one tablespoon at a time, until it comes together.
4. Turn the dough out onto a lightly floured surface and knead it gently for a minute or two until smooth.
5. Divide the dough into small portions and roll each portion into a ball. Then, flatten each ball slightly to form a disc shape.
6. Heat vegetable oil in a deep fryer or heavy-bottomed pot to 350°F (175°C).

7. Fry the doughnuts in batches, being careful not to overcrowd the pot, until golden brown and cooked through, about 2-3 minutes per side.
8. Use a slotted spoon to remove the doughnuts from the oil and transfer them to a paper towel-lined plate to drain excess oil.
9. In a small bowl, whisk together the confectioners' sugar, water, and vanilla extract to make the glaze. Add more water if needed to achieve a smooth, pourable consistency.
10. Dip each doughnut into the glaze, allowing any excess to drip off, then place them on a wire rack set over a baking sheet to catch any drips.
11. Let the glaze set for a few minutes before serving the rosquillas.
12. Serve the rosquillas as a delicious sweet treat with coffee, tea, or hot chocolate.

These homemade rosquillas are soft, fluffy, and utterly irresistible, perfect for enjoying as a snack or dessert any time of day!

Pestiños (Honey Fritters)

Ingredients:

For the Dough:

- 4 cups (500g) all-purpose flour
- 1 teaspoon baking powder
- Pinch of salt
- 1/4 cup (60ml) white wine or dry sherry
- 1/4 cup (60ml) olive oil
- 1/4 cup (60ml) orange juice
- Zest of 1 orange
- 1 teaspoon ground anise seeds (optional)
- Vegetable oil, for frying

For the Honey Syrup:

- 1 cup (240ml) honey
- 1/2 cup (120ml) water
- Zest of 1 lemon
- Zest of 1 orange
- 1 cinnamon stick
- Pinch of ground cinnamon

Instructions:

1. In a large mixing bowl, combine the flour, baking powder, and salt.
2. In a separate bowl, whisk together the white wine, olive oil, orange juice, orange zest, and ground anise seeds (if using).
3. Gradually add the wet ingredients to the dry ingredients, mixing until a smooth dough forms. You may need to knead the dough lightly with your hands to fully incorporate the ingredients.
4. Cover the dough with plastic wrap and let it rest at room temperature for 30 minutes to 1 hour.

5. While the dough is resting, prepare the honey syrup. In a saucepan, combine the honey, water, lemon zest, orange zest, cinnamon stick, and ground cinnamon. Bring to a simmer over medium heat, then reduce the heat to low and let the syrup simmer gently for 5-10 minutes. Remove from heat and let it cool slightly.
6. On a lightly floured surface, roll out the dough to about 1/8 inch thickness. Use a knife or pastry cutter to cut the dough into rectangles or diamond shapes.
7. Heat vegetable oil in a deep fryer or heavy-bottomed pot to 350°F (175°C).
8. Carefully fry the pestiños in batches until golden brown and crispy, about 2-3 minutes per side. Use a slotted spoon to transfer them to a paper towel-lined plate to drain excess oil.
9. While the pestiños are still warm, dip them into the warm honey syrup, coating them thoroughly. Use a slotted spoon or fork to remove them from the syrup and transfer them to a wire rack to cool and allow any excess syrup to drip off.
10. Let the pestiños cool completely before serving.
11. Serve the pestiños as a delicious sweet treat, drizzling any remaining honey syrup over the top if desired.

These homemade pestiños are a delightful indulgence, perfect for enjoying with a cup of coffee or tea during festive occasions or as a special dessert anytime!

Torrijas (Spanish French Toast)

Ingredients:

- 1 loaf of day-old bread, preferably a dense bread like brioche or baguette
- 4 cups (1 liter) whole milk
- 1 cinnamon stick
- Zest of 1 lemon
- Zest of 1 orange
- 1 cup (200g) granulated sugar
- 4 large eggs
- Vegetable oil, for frying
- Ground cinnamon, for dusting (optional)

Instructions:

1. Cut the day-old bread into thick slices, about 1 inch thick. You can trim the crusts off if desired, but leaving them on adds texture.
2. In a large saucepan, combine the milk, cinnamon stick, lemon zest, orange zest, and half of the granulated sugar. Heat over medium heat until the mixture just begins to simmer, then remove from heat and let it steep for 10-15 minutes to infuse the flavors.
3. In a shallow dish, beat the eggs together.
4. Dip each bread slice into the milk mixture, allowing it to soak for a few seconds on each side until fully saturated but not falling apart.
5. Heat vegetable oil in a large skillet or frying pan over medium heat. You want enough oil to come about halfway up the sides of the bread slices.
6. Once the oil is hot, carefully add the soaked bread slices to the skillet, working in batches if necessary to avoid overcrowding the pan. Fry the torrijas until golden brown and crispy on each side, about 2-3 minutes per side.
7. Use a slotted spatula to transfer the fried torrijas to a plate lined with paper towels to drain any excess oil.
8. While the torrijas are still warm, sprinkle them with the remaining granulated sugar and, if desired, ground cinnamon.
9. Serve the torrijas warm or at room temperature, as they are or accompanied by a drizzle of honey or syrup.

10. Enjoy these delicious Spanish French toast as a sweet and comforting dessert or breakfast treat!

Torrijas can be made ahead of time and stored in the refrigerator. Simply reheat them in the oven or microwave before serving. They're best enjoyed fresh but can be kept for a day or two in the fridge.

Tarta de Queso (Spanish Cheesecake)

Ingredients:

For the Crust:

- 1 1/2 cups (150g) graham cracker crumbs
- 1/4 cup (50g) granulated sugar
- 1/2 cup (115g) unsalted butter, melted

For the Filling:

- 24 oz (680g) cream cheese, softened
- 1 cup (200g) granulated sugar
- 4 large eggs
- 1/4 cup (60ml) heavy cream
- 1 tablespoon all-purpose flour
- 1 teaspoon vanilla extract
- Zest of 1 lemon (optional)

Instructions:

1. Preheat your oven to 325°F (160°C). Grease a 9-inch springform pan and line the bottom with parchment paper.
2. In a mixing bowl, combine the graham cracker crumbs, granulated sugar, and melted butter. Mix until well combined and the mixture resembles wet sand.
3. Press the crumb mixture firmly and evenly into the bottom of the prepared springform pan. Use the bottom of a measuring cup or glass to help compact the crust.
4. In a large mixing bowl, beat the cream cheese and granulated sugar together until smooth and creamy.
5. Add the eggs one at a time, beating well after each addition.
6. Stir in the heavy cream, flour, vanilla extract, and lemon zest (if using), mixing until everything is well combined and the batter is smooth.
7. Pour the cheesecake filling over the prepared crust in the springform pan, spreading it out evenly with a spatula.

8. Bake the cheesecake in the preheated oven for 50-60 minutes, or until the edges are set and the center is slightly jiggly.
9. Turn off the oven and leave the cheesecake inside with the door slightly ajar for about 1 hour to cool gradually.
10. Once cooled, refrigerate the cheesecake for at least 4 hours or overnight to chill and set completely.
11. Before serving, run a knife around the edges of the springform pan to loosen the cheesecake. Remove the sides of the pan.
12. Serve slices of Tarta de Queso chilled, optionally garnished with fresh berries or a dusting of powdered sugar.

Enjoy the rich and creamy texture of this Spanish Cheesecake, with its slightly caramelized top and indulgent flavor. It's sure to be a hit at any gathering or as a special treat for yourself!

Mantecados (Spanish Christmas Cookies)

Ingredients:

- 2 cups (250g) all-purpose flour
- 3/4 cup (150g) granulated sugar
- 1/2 cup (115g) lard or vegetable shortening
- 1/4 cup (60ml) brandy or rum (optional)
- 1 teaspoon ground cinnamon
- 1/4 teaspoon ground cloves
- Zest of 1 lemon
- Pinch of salt
- Confectioners' sugar, for dusting

Instructions:

1. Preheat your oven to 350°F (175°C). Line a baking sheet with parchment paper.
2. In a large mixing bowl, combine the flour, granulated sugar, ground cinnamon, ground cloves, lemon zest, and salt.
3. Add the lard or vegetable shortening to the dry ingredients. Use your fingers or a pastry cutter to mix until the mixture resembles coarse crumbs and the fat is evenly distributed.
4. If using, add the brandy or rum to the mixture and mix until it comes together to form a dough. If the dough is too dry, you can add a little more brandy or rum, one tablespoon at a time, until it holds together.
5. Divide the dough into small portions and shape each portion into a ball or cylinder shape. You can also use cookie cutters to shape the dough into different shapes if desired.
6. Place the shaped mantecados on the prepared baking sheet, spacing them slightly apart.
7. Bake the mantecados in the preheated oven for 15-20 minutes, or until they are lightly golden brown around the edges.
8. Remove the mantecados from the oven and let them cool on the baking sheet for a few minutes before transferring them to a wire rack to cool completely.
9. Once cooled, dust the mantecados generously with confectioners' sugar.
10. Serve the mantecados as a delicious sweet treat with coffee or hot chocolate, or package them in decorative boxes to give as gifts during the holiday season.

Enjoy these classic Spanish Christmas cookies with their crumbly texture and aromatic flavors, perfect for celebrating the holiday season with family and friends!

Alfajores (Spanish Sandwich Cookies)

Ingredients:

For the Cookies:

- 1 cup (225g) unsalted butter, softened
- 1/2 cup (100g) granulated sugar
- 2 cups (250g) all-purpose flour
- 1 cup (125g) cornstarch
- 1 teaspoon baking powder
- 1/2 teaspoon baking soda
- 1/4 teaspoon salt
- 1 teaspoon vanilla extract
- Zest of 1 lemon (optional)
- Dulce de leche, for filling
- Powdered sugar, for dusting

Instructions:

1. Preheat your oven to 350°F (175°C). Line a baking sheet with parchment paper.
2. In a large mixing bowl, cream together the softened butter and granulated sugar until light and fluffy.
3. In a separate bowl, sift together the all-purpose flour, cornstarch, baking powder, baking soda, and salt.
4. Gradually add the dry ingredients to the creamed butter and sugar mixture, mixing until a soft dough forms. Add the vanilla extract and lemon zest (if using) and mix until well combined.
5. Roll out the dough on a lightly floured surface to about 1/4 inch thickness. Use a cookie cutter to cut out rounds of dough.
6. Place the cut-out cookies onto the prepared baking sheet, spacing them slightly apart.
7. Bake the cookies in the preheated oven for 10-12 minutes, or until they are just beginning to turn golden brown around the edges.
8. Remove the cookies from the oven and let them cool on the baking sheet for a few minutes before transferring them to a wire rack to cool completely.

9. Once the cookies have cooled completely, spread a layer of dulce de leche onto the bottom side of half of the cookies.
10. Place another cookie on top of each dulce de leche-covered cookie to form a sandwich.
11. Dust the alfajores generously with powdered sugar before serving.
12. Serve the alfajores as a delicious sweet treat with coffee or tea, or package them in decorative boxes to give as gifts.

Enjoy these delightful Spanish sandwich cookies with their buttery shortbread texture and sweet dulce de leche filling, perfect for indulging in a taste of Spain at home!

Bunuelos de Viento (Spanish Wind Fritters)

Ingredients:

- 1 cup (125g) all-purpose flour
- 1 cup (240ml) water
- 1/4 cup (50g) unsalted butter
- 4 large eggs
- Zest of 1 lemon
- Pinch of salt
- Vegetable oil, for frying
- Powdered sugar, for dusting

Instructions:

1. In a saucepan, bring the water, butter, lemon zest, and salt to a boil over medium heat.
2. Reduce the heat to low and add the flour all at once. Stir vigorously with a wooden spoon until the mixture forms a smooth dough and pulls away from the sides of the pan, about 1-2 minutes. Remove from heat and let it cool slightly.
3. Transfer the dough to a mixing bowl and let it cool for a few minutes.
4. Add the eggs to the dough, one at a time, mixing well after each addition. The dough will be sticky at first but will come together as you mix.
5. Heat vegetable oil in a deep fryer or heavy-bottomed pot to 350°F (175°C).
6. Using two spoons or a small ice cream scoop, drop spoonfuls of dough into the hot oil, being careful not to overcrowd the pot. Fry the bunuelos in batches until golden brown and puffed up, about 3-4 minutes, turning them occasionally for even browning.
7. Use a slotted spoon to transfer the fried bunuelos to a plate lined with paper towels to drain excess oil.
8. Once all the bunuelos are fried and drained, dust them generously with powdered sugar.
9. Serve the bunuelos de viento warm as a delicious sweet treat.

These fluffy and airy Spanish wind fritters are perfect for enjoying with a cup of coffee or hot chocolate during festive occasions or as a special dessert anytime!

Natillas (Spanish Custard)

Ingredients:

- 4 cups (1 liter) whole milk
- 6 large egg yolks
- 1 cup (200g) granulated sugar
- 1/4 cup (30g) cornstarch
- Zest of 1 lemon
- 1 cinnamon stick
- Ground cinnamon, for garnish (optional)

Instructions:

1. In a saucepan, combine the milk, lemon zest, and cinnamon stick. Heat over medium heat until it just begins to simmer. Remove from heat and let it steep for 10-15 minutes to infuse the flavors. Remove the lemon zest and cinnamon stick.
2. In a mixing bowl, whisk together the egg yolks, granulated sugar, and cornstarch until smooth and creamy.
3. Gradually pour the warm milk mixture into the egg yolk mixture, whisking constantly to prevent curdling.
4. Pour the mixture back into the saucepan and cook over medium heat, stirring constantly, until it thickens and coats the back of a spoon, about 5-7 minutes. Do not let it boil.
5. Once thickened, remove the saucepan from the heat and strain the mixture through a fine mesh sieve into a clean bowl to remove any lumps.
6. Transfer the natillas to individual serving dishes or ramekins. Let them cool to room temperature, then cover with plastic wrap and refrigerate for at least 2-3 hours, or until set.
7. Before serving, sprinkle the top of each natilla with ground cinnamon if desired.
8. Serve the natillas chilled as a delicious and creamy dessert.

Natillas are a delightful Spanish dessert, perfect for enjoying after a meal or as a sweet treat any time of day. The combination of cinnamon and lemon adds a lovely aroma and flavor to this classic custard.

Magdalenas (Spanish Lemon Muffins)

Ingredients:

- 2 cups (250g) all-purpose flour
- 1 1/2 teaspoons baking powder
- 1/4 teaspoon salt
- 3 large eggs, at room temperature
- 1 cup (200g) granulated sugar
- 1/2 cup (120ml) vegetable oil
- 1/4 cup (60ml) milk
- Zest of 2 lemons
- 1 teaspoon vanilla extract
- Powdered sugar, for dusting (optional)

Instructions:

1. Preheat your oven to 350°F (175°C). Line a muffin tin with paper liners or grease the cups with butter or cooking spray.
2. In a mixing bowl, sift together the all-purpose flour, baking powder, and salt. Set aside.
3. In another mixing bowl, beat the eggs and granulated sugar together until light and fluffy.
4. Gradually add the vegetable oil while continuing to beat the mixture until well combined.
5. Stir in the milk, lemon zest, and vanilla extract until evenly incorporated.
6. Gradually add the dry ingredients to the wet ingredients, mixing until just combined. Be careful not to overmix, as this can result in tough muffins.
7. Spoon the batter into the prepared muffin tin, filling each cup about 3/4 full.
8. Bake the magdalenas in the preheated oven for 15-20 minutes, or until they are lightly golden brown on top and a toothpick inserted into the center comes out clean.
9. Remove the muffins from the oven and let them cool in the tin for a few minutes before transferring them to a wire rack to cool completely.
10. Once cooled, dust the tops of the magdalenas with powdered sugar if desired.

11. Serve the magdalenas as a delicious breakfast treat or afternoon snack, accompanied by coffee or tea.

These Spanish lemon muffins are sure to become a favorite in your household with their light and fluffy texture and refreshing citrus flavor. Enjoy them fresh out of the oven for the ultimate indulgence!

Pastissets (Spanish Pastry Cookies)

Ingredients:

For the Dough:

- 2 cups (250g) all-purpose flour
- 1/2 cup (100g) granulated sugar
- 1/2 cup (115g) unsalted butter, softened
- 2 large eggs
- 1 teaspoon baking powder
- Zest of 1 lemon
- Pinch of salt

For the Filling:

- Your choice of fruit preserves or almond paste

Instructions:

1. In a mixing bowl, cream together the softened butter and granulated sugar until light and fluffy.
2. Add the eggs one at a time, beating well after each addition.
3. Stir in the lemon zest.
4. In a separate bowl, sift together the all-purpose flour, baking powder, and salt.
5. Gradually add the dry ingredients to the wet ingredients, mixing until a dough forms. If the dough is too sticky, you can add a little more flour.
6. Wrap the dough in plastic wrap and refrigerate it for at least 30 minutes to firm up.
7. Preheat your oven to 350°F (175°C). Line a baking sheet with parchment paper.
8. Roll out the chilled dough on a lightly floured surface to about 1/4 inch thickness. Use a round cookie cutter to cut out circles of dough.
9. Place a small spoonful of fruit preserves or almond paste in the center of each dough circle.
10. Fold the dough over the filling to form a half-moon shape, then use a fork to crimp the edges closed.

11. Place the filled pastissets on the prepared baking sheet, spacing them slightly apart.
12. Bake the pastissets in the preheated oven for 12-15 minutes, or until they are lightly golden brown around the edges.
13. Remove the pastissets from the oven and let them cool on the baking sheet for a few minutes before transferring them to a wire rack to cool completely.
14. Once cooled, serve the pastissets as a delicious sweet treat with coffee or tea.

These Spanish pastry cookies are perfect for enjoying as a snack or dessert, with their tender crust and flavorful filling. Customize them with your favorite fruit preserves or almond paste for a delightful treat!

Miguelitos (Puff Pastry Desserts)

Ingredients:

- 1 sheet of frozen puff pastry, thawed
- 1 cup (240ml) heavy cream
- 2 tablespoons powdered sugar, plus extra for dusting
- 1 teaspoon vanilla extract

Instructions:

1. Preheat your oven to 400°F (200°C). Line a baking sheet with parchment paper.
2. Roll out the thawed puff pastry sheet on a lightly floured surface to about 1/4 inch thickness.
3. Use a sharp knife or pizza cutter to cut the puff pastry into small rectangles, about 2 inches wide and 4 inches long.
4. Place the puff pastry rectangles on the prepared baking sheet, leaving some space between each one.
5. Bake the puff pastry rectangles in the preheated oven for 15-20 minutes, or until they are puffed and golden brown.
6. While the puff pastry is baking, prepare the sweet cream filling. In a mixing bowl, whip the heavy cream, powdered sugar, and vanilla extract together until stiff peaks form.
7. Once the puff pastry rectangles are baked and cooled, use a sharp knife to slice each one horizontally, creating a top and bottom layer.
8. Spoon a dollop of sweet cream filling onto the bottom half of each puff pastry rectangle.
9. Place the top half of each puff pastry rectangle over the sweet cream filling to create a sandwich.
10. Dust the top of each miguelito with powdered sugar.
11. Serve the miguelitos as a delicious sweet treat with coffee or tea.

These puff pastry desserts are simple to make yet incredibly delicious, with their flaky layers and creamy filling. Enjoy them fresh out of the oven for a delightful indulgence!

Tocino de Cielo (Spanish Egg Yolk Flan)

Ingredients:

- 10 egg yolks
- 1 cup (200g) granulated sugar
- 1/2 cup (120ml) water
- Caramel sauce (optional, for serving)

Instructions:

1. Preheat your oven to 350°F (175°C). Prepare a bain-marie (water bath) by placing a baking dish filled with water in the oven.
2. In a saucepan, combine the sugar and water over medium heat. Stir until the sugar has dissolved completely.
3. Let the sugar syrup cook without stirring until it reaches a light golden color, about 5-7 minutes. Be careful not to let it burn.
4. Once the caramel is ready, remove it from heat and pour it into individual ramekins or a large baking dish. Tilt the ramekins or dish to evenly coat the bottom with caramel. Set aside to cool and harden.
5. In a large mixing bowl, whisk the egg yolks until well combined.
6. Gradually pour the egg yolks into the caramel-coated ramekins or baking dish.
7. Place the ramekins or baking dish into the bain-marie in the preheated oven.
8. Bake for about 30-40 minutes, or until the tocino de cielo is set but still jiggly in the center.
9. Remove the ramekins or baking dish from the oven and let the tocino de cielo cool to room temperature.
10. Once cooled, refrigerate the tocino de cielo for at least 2 hours, or until fully chilled.
11. To serve, run a knife around the edges of the ramekins or baking dish to loosen the tocino de cielo. Invert the ramekins or dish onto serving plates to release the flan, or serve directly from the dish.
12. Optionally, drizzle caramel sauce over the tocino de cielo before serving.

Tocino de cielo is a deliciously indulgent dessert that's perfect for special occasions or whenever you're craving something sweet and decadent. Enjoy its rich flavor and smooth texture!

Galletas Maria (Spanish Maria Biscuits)

Ingredients:

- 2 cups (250g) all-purpose flour
- 1/2 cup (100g) granulated sugar
- 1/2 cup (115g) unsalted butter, softened
- 1 large egg
- 1 teaspoon baking powder
- 1/2 teaspoon vanilla extract
- Pinch of salt

Instructions:

1. Preheat your oven to 350°F (175°C). Line a baking sheet with parchment paper.
2. In a mixing bowl, cream together the softened butter and granulated sugar until light and fluffy.
3. Add the egg and vanilla extract to the butter mixture, and beat until well combined.
4. In a separate bowl, sift together the all-purpose flour, baking powder, and salt.
5. Gradually add the dry ingredients to the wet ingredients, mixing until a dough forms. If the dough is too sticky, you can add a little more flour.
6. Roll out the dough on a lightly floured surface to about 1/4 inch thickness.
7. Use a round cookie cutter or the rim of a glass to cut out circles of dough.
8. Place the dough circles on the prepared baking sheet, spacing them slightly apart.
9. Prick each dough circle several times with a fork to prevent them from puffing up too much during baking.
10. Bake the galletas María in the preheated oven for 10-12 minutes, or until they are lightly golden brown around the edges.
11. Remove the biscuits from the oven and let them cool on the baking sheet for a few minutes before transferring them to a wire rack to cool completely.
12. Once cooled, store the galletas María in an airtight container at room temperature.

These homemade galletas María are perfect for enjoying as a snack or with your favorite hot beverage. They have a delicate texture and a subtle sweetness that makes them irresistible!

Empanada Gallega (Galician Meat Pie)

Ingredients:

For the Dough:

- 4 cups (500g) all-purpose flour
- 1 teaspoon salt
- 1 cup (230g) unsalted butter, cold and diced
- 1/2 cup (120ml) cold water

For the Filling:

- 1 lb (450g) ground beef or pork
- 1 onion, finely chopped
- 2 cloves garlic, minced
- 1 red bell pepper, diced
- 1 green bell pepper, diced
- 1 teaspoon paprika
- 1/2 teaspoon cumin
- Salt and pepper to taste
- Olive oil for cooking
- 2 hard-boiled eggs, sliced
- Optional: pitted olives

Instructions:

1. In a large mixing bowl, combine the flour and salt. Add the cold diced butter and rub it into the flour using your fingertips until the mixture resembles coarse breadcrumbs.
2. Gradually add the cold water, mixing with a fork until the dough comes together. Shape the dough into a ball, wrap it in plastic wrap, and refrigerate for at least 30 minutes.
3. Meanwhile, prepare the filling. Heat some olive oil in a large skillet over medium heat. Add the chopped onion and cook until translucent.
4. Add the minced garlic and diced bell peppers to the skillet, and cook until softened.

5. Add the ground beef or pork to the skillet and cook until browned, breaking it up with a spoon as it cooks.
6. Season the filling with paprika, cumin, salt, and pepper to taste. Cook for a few more minutes, then remove from heat and let it cool slightly.
7. Preheat your oven to 375°F (190°C). Grease a baking sheet or line it with parchment paper.
8. Divide the dough into two portions, one slightly larger than the other. Roll out the larger portion of dough on a floured surface to fit the bottom of your baking sheet.
9. Transfer the rolled-out dough to the prepared baking sheet, pressing it down gently to fit.
10. Spread the cooled meat filling evenly over the dough, leaving a border around the edges.
11. Arrange the sliced hard-boiled eggs (and olives if using) over the meat filling.
12. Roll out the remaining portion of dough to fit over the filling, then place it on top of the meat mixture. Press the edges of the top and bottom crusts together to seal.
13. Use a sharp knife to make small slits in the top crust to allow steam to escape during baking.
14. Bake the empanada in the preheated oven for 30-40 minutes, or until the crust is golden brown.
15. Let the empanada cool slightly before slicing and serving. It can be enjoyed warm or at room temperature.

Empanada Gallega is a delicious and satisfying dish that's perfect for sharing with family and friends. Enjoy the flavors of Galicia with this classic meat pie!

Ensaïmada (Spanish Sweet Pastry)

Ingredients:

For the Dough:

- 4 cups (500g) all-purpose flour
- 1/2 cup (100g) granulated sugar
- 1/2 cup (120ml) warm water
- 2 1/4 teaspoons (1 packet) active dry yeast
- 3 large eggs, at room temperature
- 1/2 cup (115g) unsalted butter, melted
- Zest of 1 lemon
- Pinch of salt

For the Filling (optional):

- 1/2 cup (100g) granulated sugar
- 1/2 cup (115g) unsalted butter, softened
- Powdered sugar, for dusting

Instructions:

1. In a small bowl, combine the warm water and active dry yeast. Let it sit for about 5-10 minutes, or until foamy.
2. In a large mixing bowl, combine the flour, granulated sugar, lemon zest, and salt. Make a well in the center and add the yeast mixture, melted butter, and eggs.
3. Mix everything together until a dough forms. Turn the dough out onto a floured surface and knead it for about 10-15 minutes, or until smooth and elastic.
4. Place the dough in a greased bowl, cover it with a clean kitchen towel, and let it rise in a warm place for 1-2 hours, or until doubled in size.
5. Punch down the dough to release the air, then divide it into equal portions (depending on the size of ensaïmada you want to make).
6. Roll out each portion of dough into a thin rectangle.
7. Spread the softened butter evenly over the surface of each rectangle of dough, then sprinkle with granulated sugar.
8. Roll up each rectangle of dough tightly, starting from the long side, to form a long log.

9. Take one of the logs and coil it into a spiral shape, tucking the end underneath. Repeat with the remaining logs.
10. Place the coiled dough on a baking sheet lined with parchment paper, cover it with a clean kitchen towel, and let it rise for another 30-60 minutes.
11. Preheat your oven to 350°F (175°C).
12. Bake the ensaïmada in the preheated oven for 20-25 minutes, or until golden brown and cooked through.
13. Remove the ensaïmada from the oven and let it cool slightly on the baking sheet.
14. Once cooled, dust the ensaïmada generously with powdered sugar.
15. Serve the ensaïmada warm or at room temperature.

Ensaïmada is best enjoyed fresh, with a cup of coffee or hot chocolate. Its delicate layers and sweet flavor make it a delightful treat for any occasion!

Polvorones de Almendra (Almond Powder Cookies)

Ingredients:

- 2 cups (250g) all-purpose flour
- 1 cup (100g) ground almonds (almond flour)
- 3/4 cup (150g) granulated sugar
- 1 cup (230g) unsalted butter, softened
- 1 teaspoon vanilla extract
- 1/4 teaspoon ground cinnamon (optional)
- Powdered sugar, for dusting

Instructions:

1. Preheat your oven to 350°F (175°C). Line a baking sheet with parchment paper.
2. In a large mixing bowl, combine the all-purpose flour, ground almonds, granulated sugar, and ground cinnamon (if using).
3. Add the softened butter and vanilla extract to the dry ingredients. Use your hands or a pastry cutter to mix until the dough comes together and forms a crumbly texture.
4. Once the dough starts to come together, transfer it to a clean work surface and knead it gently until smooth. Be careful not to overwork the dough.
5. Divide the dough into smaller portions and shape each portion into a round disc or cylinder. You can also use cookie cutters to shape the dough into different shapes if desired.
6. Place the shaped cookies onto the prepared baking sheet, spacing them slightly apart.
7. Bake the cookies in the preheated oven for 12-15 minutes, or until they are just beginning to turn golden brown around the edges.
8. Remove the cookies from the oven and let them cool on the baking sheet for a few minutes before transferring them to a wire rack to cool completely.
9. Once cooled, dust the polvorones generously with powdered sugar.
10. Serve the polvorones de almendra as a delicious sweet treat with coffee or tea.

These almond powder cookies are perfect for enjoying as a snack or dessert, with their crumbly texture and rich almond flavor. Enjoy their melt-in-your-mouth goodness!

Cabello de Ángel (Angel Hair Pastry)

Ingredients:

- 1 medium spaghetti squash or pumpkin
- Granulated sugar
- Water
- Lemon zest (optional)
- Cinnamon stick (optional)

Instructions:

1. Preheat your oven to 375°F (190°C). Line a baking sheet with parchment paper.
2. Cut the spaghetti squash or pumpkin in half lengthwise and remove the seeds and fibers from the center.
3. Place the squash or pumpkin halves cut side down on the prepared baking sheet.
4. Bake in the preheated oven for about 40-50 minutes, or until the flesh is tender when pierced with a fork.
5. Remove the squash or pumpkin from the oven and let it cool slightly until you can handle it comfortably.
6. Use a fork to scrape the flesh of the squash or pumpkin into spaghetti-like strands. Alternatively, you can use a spoon to scoop out the flesh and shred it into thin strands.
7. In a large saucepan, combine equal parts of shredded squash or pumpkin and granulated sugar. Add enough water to cover the mixture.
8. If desired, add lemon zest and a cinnamon stick to the saucepan for extra flavor.
9. Bring the mixture to a simmer over medium heat, stirring occasionally.
10. Reduce the heat to low and let the mixture cook gently, stirring occasionally, until the liquid evaporates and the squash or pumpkin becomes translucent and jam-like in consistency. This may take about 1-2 hours.
11. Once the cabello de ángel is ready, remove it from the heat and let it cool completely.
12. Transfer the cabello de ángel to sterilized jars or containers for storage.

You can use cabello de ángel as a filling for pastries like empanadas or ensaimadas, or as a topping for desserts like flan or ice cream. Enjoy this sweet and fragrant Spanish delicacy!

Pudin de Pan (Spanish Bread Pudding)

Ingredients:

- 6 cups (about 300g) stale bread, cut into cubes
- 4 cups (960ml) whole milk
- 4 large eggs
- 1 cup (200g) granulated sugar
- Zest of 1 lemon
- 1 teaspoon vanilla extract
- 1/2 teaspoon ground cinnamon
- 1/4 teaspoon ground nutmeg
- Pinch of salt
- Raisins or other dried fruits (optional)
- Caramel sauce or powdered sugar, for serving (optional)

Instructions:

1. Preheat your oven to 350°F (175°C). Grease a baking dish with butter or cooking spray.
2. Place the bread cubes in a large mixing bowl.
3. In a separate saucepan, heat the milk over medium heat until it just begins to simmer. Remove from heat and let it cool slightly.
4. In another mixing bowl, whisk together the eggs, granulated sugar, lemon zest, vanilla extract, ground cinnamon, ground nutmeg, and a pinch of salt until well combined.
5. Gradually pour the warm milk into the egg mixture, whisking constantly to temper the eggs.
6. Pour the custard mixture over the bread cubes in the mixing bowl. Add the raisins or other dried fruits if using. Gently toss until the bread is evenly coated and soaked in the custard mixture.
7. Let the bread mixture sit for about 10-15 minutes to allow the bread to absorb the custard.
8. Transfer the bread mixture to the prepared baking dish, spreading it out evenly.
9. Bake the pudding in the preheated oven for 40-50 minutes, or until the top is golden brown and the custard is set.
10. Remove the pudding from the oven and let it cool slightly before serving.

11. Serve the pudin de pan warm, drizzled with caramel sauce or dusted with powdered sugar if desired.

Pudin de pan is a comforting and versatile dessert that's perfect for using up leftover bread. Enjoy it as a cozy treat on its own or with your favorite sauce or toppings!

Bizcocho de Chocolate (Spanish Chocolate Cake)

Ingredients:

- 1 3/4 cups (220g) all-purpose flour
- 3/4 cup (65g) unsweetened cocoa powder
- 1 1/2 teaspoons baking powder
- 1/2 teaspoon baking soda
- 1/2 teaspoon salt
- 1 cup (200g) granulated sugar
- 3/4 cup (180ml) vegetable oil
- 3 large eggs, at room temperature
- 1 teaspoon vanilla extract
- 1 cup (240ml) buttermilk, at room temperature
- 1/2 cup (120ml) hot water
- Powdered sugar or chocolate ganache, for topping (optional)

Instructions:

1. Preheat your oven to 350°F (175°C). Grease and flour a 9-inch (23cm) round cake pan or line it with parchment paper.
2. In a large mixing bowl, sift together the all-purpose flour, cocoa powder, baking powder, baking soda, and salt. Set aside.
3. In another mixing bowl, whisk together the granulated sugar, vegetable oil, eggs, and vanilla extract until well combined.
4. Gradually add the dry ingredients to the wet ingredients, alternating with the buttermilk, beginning and ending with the dry ingredients. Mix until just combined, being careful not to overmix.
5. Gradually add the hot water to the batter, mixing until smooth. The batter will be thin, but this is normal.
6. Pour the batter into the prepared cake pan and spread it out evenly.
7. Bake in the preheated oven for 30-35 minutes, or until a toothpick inserted into the center comes out clean.
8. Remove the cake from the oven and let it cool in the pan for about 10 minutes.
9. Carefully transfer the cake to a wire rack to cool completely.
10. Once cooled, you can dust the cake with powdered sugar or drizzle it with chocolate ganache for extra indulgence.

11. Slice and serve the bizcocho de chocolate as desired.

This Spanish chocolate cake is perfect for any occasion, from birthdays to special celebrations, or simply as a sweet treat to enjoy with a cup of coffee or tea. Enjoy its rich chocolate flavor and moist texture!

Tortas de Aceite (Spanish Olive Oil Biscuits)

Ingredients:

- 2 cups (250g) all-purpose flour, plus extra for dusting
- 1/2 teaspoon baking powder
- 1/4 teaspoon salt
- 1/2 cup (120ml) extra virgin olive oil
- 1/4 cup (60ml) dry white wine
- 1/4 cup (50g) granulated sugar
- 1 teaspoon anise seeds
- 1 tablespoon sesame seeds

Instructions:

1. Preheat your oven to 375°F (190°C). Line a baking sheet with parchment paper.
2. In a large mixing bowl, sift together the all-purpose flour, baking powder, and salt.
3. In a separate bowl, mix together the olive oil, dry white wine, and granulated sugar until well combined.
4. Gradually add the wet ingredients to the dry ingredients, mixing until a smooth dough forms.
5. Knead the dough lightly on a floured surface for a few minutes until it becomes elastic.
6. Divide the dough into small portions, about the size of a golf ball, and roll each portion into a thin circle, about 1/8 inch thick.
7. Place the dough circles on the prepared baking sheet.
8. Sprinkle the anise seeds and sesame seeds evenly over the dough circles, pressing them lightly into the surface.
9. Bake in the preheated oven for 10-12 minutes, or until the tortas de aceite are golden brown and crisp.
10. Remove the biscuits from the oven and let them cool on the baking sheet for a few minutes before transferring them to a wire rack to cool completely.
11. Once cooled, serve the tortas de aceite as a delightful snack or dessert with a cup of coffee or tea.

These Spanish olive oil biscuits are light, crisp, and subtly sweet, making them perfect for enjoying on their own or with your favorite spread. Enjoy the unique flavor of olive oil in this traditional Andalusian treat!

Crema de Calabaza (Spanish Pumpkin Cream)

Ingredients:

- 1 small pumpkin or butternut squash, peeled, seeded, and diced (about 4 cups)
- 1 onion, chopped
- 2 cloves garlic, minced
- 1 potato, peeled and diced
- 4 cups (1 liter) vegetable or chicken broth
- 1 cup (240ml) heavy cream
- 2 tablespoons olive oil
- Salt and pepper, to taste
- Fresh parsley or cilantro, for garnish (optional)

Instructions:

1. Heat the olive oil in a large pot over medium heat. Add the chopped onion and cook until soft and translucent, about 5 minutes.
2. Add the minced garlic to the pot and cook for an additional 1-2 minutes, until fragrant.
3. Add the diced pumpkin or butternut squash and potato to the pot. Season with salt and pepper to taste. Cook for 5 minutes, stirring occasionally.
4. Pour the vegetable or chicken broth into the pot and bring the mixture to a boil. Reduce the heat to low, cover, and simmer for 20-25 minutes, or until the pumpkin and potato are tender.
5. Once the vegetables are cooked through, remove the pot from the heat. Use an immersion blender to puree the soup until smooth and creamy. Alternatively, you can transfer the soup in batches to a blender and blend until smooth, then return it to the pot.
6. Return the pot to the stove over low heat. Stir in the heavy cream and heat the soup gently until warmed through, about 5 minutes.
7. Taste the soup and adjust the seasoning with more salt and pepper if needed.
8. Ladle the crema de calabaza into bowls and garnish with fresh parsley or cilantro, if desired.
9. Serve the soup hot with crusty bread or crackers on the side.

This Spanish pumpkin cream is velvety smooth, rich, and full of flavor. It's the perfect comforting dish to enjoy on a chilly day. Enjoy!

Torta de Manzana (Spanish Apple Cake)

Ingredients:

- 2 cups (250g) all-purpose flour
- 1 teaspoon baking powder
- 1/2 teaspoon baking soda
- 1/2 teaspoon ground cinnamon
- 1/4 teaspoon ground nutmeg
- Pinch of salt
- 1/2 cup (115g) unsalted butter, softened
- 3/4 cup (150g) granulated sugar
- 2 large eggs, at room temperature
- 1 teaspoon vanilla extract
- 1/2 cup (120ml) milk
- 2 medium apples, peeled, cored, and thinly sliced
- 2 tablespoons granulated sugar mixed with 1 teaspoon ground cinnamon, for topping

Instructions:

1. Preheat your oven to 350°F (175°C). Grease and flour a 9-inch (23cm) round cake pan.
2. In a medium bowl, sift together the all-purpose flour, baking powder, baking soda, ground cinnamon, ground nutmeg, and salt. Set aside.
3. In a large mixing bowl, cream together the softened butter and granulated sugar until light and fluffy.
4. Add the eggs one at a time, beating well after each addition. Stir in the vanilla extract.
5. Gradually add the dry ingredients to the wet ingredients, alternating with the milk, beginning and ending with the dry ingredients. Mix until just combined.
6. Pour the batter into the prepared cake pan and spread it out evenly.
7. Arrange the thinly sliced apples on top of the batter in a decorative pattern.
8. Sprinkle the cinnamon-sugar mixture evenly over the apples.
9. Bake in the preheated oven for 40-45 minutes, or until a toothpick inserted into the center comes out clean and the top is golden brown.
10. Remove the cake from the oven and let it cool in the pan for 10 minutes.

11. Carefully transfer the cake to a wire rack to cool completely before slicing and serving.

This Spanish apple cake is perfect for enjoying as a sweet treat with a cup of coffee or tea. Its tender crumb and warm spices make it a comforting dessert that's sure to please. Enjoy!

Alfajor de Medina Sidonia (Spanish Almond Cookie)

Ingredients:

For the Dough:

- 2 cups (250g) almond flour
- 1 cup (200g) granulated sugar
- 2 large eggs
- Zest of 1 lemon
- 1/2 teaspoon ground cinnamon
- Pinch of salt

For the Filling:

- Dulce de leche or caramel spread
- Powdered sugar, for dusting (optional)

Instructions:

1. Preheat your oven to 350°F (175°C). Line a baking sheet with parchment paper.
2. In a large mixing bowl, combine the almond flour, granulated sugar, lemon zest, ground cinnamon, and a pinch of salt.
3. Add the eggs to the dry ingredients and mix until a dough forms. It should be smooth and slightly sticky.
4. Divide the dough into small portions and shape each portion into a ball.
5. Place the dough balls on the prepared baking sheet, spacing them slightly apart.
6. Use your thumb or the back of a spoon to make an indentation in the center of each dough ball.
7. Fill each indentation with dulce de leche or caramel spread.
8. Bake in the preheated oven for 12-15 minutes, or until the cookies are golden brown around the edges.
9. Remove the cookies from the oven and let them cool on the baking sheet for a few minutes before transferring them to a wire rack to cool completely.
10. Once cooled, dust the alfajores with powdered sugar, if desired.

These Alfajores de Medina Sidonia are wonderfully rich and nutty, with a sweet caramel filling that adds extra indulgence. Enjoy these delightful Spanish almond cookies with a cup of coffee or tea for a delicious treat!

Yemas de Santa Teresa (Spanish Egg Yolk Confections)

Ingredients:

- 12 egg yolks
- 1 1/2 cups (300g) granulated sugar
- 1/4 cup (60ml) water
- 1/4 teaspoon lemon zest (optional)
- Powdered sugar, for dusting

Instructions:

1. In a large mixing bowl, beat the egg yolks until they are well combined and slightly thickened. Set aside.
2. In a saucepan, combine the granulated sugar, water, and lemon zest (if using) over medium heat. Stir until the sugar is completely dissolved.
3. Once the sugar has dissolved, reduce the heat to low and continue to cook the syrup until it reaches the soft-ball stage, about 235°F to 240°F (112°C to 115°C) on a candy thermometer. This will take about 8-10 minutes.
4. Once the syrup has reached the desired temperature, remove it from the heat and let it cool slightly for 1-2 minutes.
5. Slowly pour the hot syrup into the beaten egg yolks, whisking constantly to prevent the yolks from cooking.
6. Return the mixture to the saucepan and cook over low heat, stirring constantly, until it thickens and reaches the consistency of a thick custard. This will take about 10-15 minutes.
7. Once thickened, remove the mixture from the heat and let it cool completely.
8. Once cooled, roll the mixture into small balls or shape them into small cones.
9. Dust the yemas de Santa Teresa with powdered sugar.
10. Serve and enjoy these delightful Spanish egg yolk confections as a sweet treat or dessert.

These yemas de Santa Teresa are a classic Spanish delicacy, with a rich and creamy texture that melts in your mouth. They make a wonderful addition to any holiday celebration or special occasion.

Arroz con Leche (Spanish Rice Pudding)

Ingredients:

- 1 cup (200g) short-grain rice (such as Arborio or Valencia rice)
- 4 cups (960ml) whole milk
- 1 cinnamon stick
- Zest of 1 lemon
- 1/2 cup (100g) granulated sugar
- Pinch of salt
- Ground cinnamon, for garnish (optional)

Instructions:

1. Rinse the rice under cold water until the water runs clear. This helps remove excess starch and prevents the rice from becoming too sticky.
2. In a large saucepan, combine the rinsed rice, whole milk, cinnamon stick, and lemon zest. Bring the mixture to a gentle boil over medium heat, stirring occasionally to prevent the rice from sticking to the bottom of the pan.
3. Once the mixture reaches a boil, reduce the heat to low and let it simmer gently, uncovered, stirring occasionally, for about 30-40 minutes, or until the rice is tender and the mixture has thickened to your desired consistency.
4. Stir in the granulated sugar and a pinch of salt, and continue to cook for an additional 5-10 minutes, stirring frequently, until the sugar is completely dissolved and the rice pudding has reached your desired sweetness.
5. Remove the cinnamon stick and lemon zest from the rice pudding and discard them.
6. Remove the rice pudding from the heat and let it cool slightly before serving. It will continue to thicken as it cools.
7. Serve the arroz con leche warm or chilled, garnished with ground cinnamon if desired.
8. Enjoy this creamy and comforting Spanish rice pudding as a delicious dessert or snack.

Arroz con leche is a beloved Spanish dessert that's perfect for any occasion. Its creamy texture and delicate flavor make it a comforting treat that's sure to please everyone!

Tarta de Tres Leches (Spanish Three Milk Cake)

Ingredients:

For the Cake:

- 1 cup (125g) all-purpose flour
- 1 1/2 teaspoons baking powder
- 1/4 teaspoon salt
- 4 large eggs, separated
- 1 cup (200g) granulated sugar
- 1/3 cup (80ml) whole milk
- 1 teaspoon vanilla extract

For the Three Milks Mixture:

- 1 can (14 ounces) sweetened condensed milk
- 1 can (12 ounces) evaporated milk
- 1 cup (240ml) whole milk

For the Topping:

- 2 cups (480ml) heavy cream
- 2 tablespoons powdered sugar
- 1 teaspoon vanilla extract
- Ground cinnamon, for garnish (optional)

Instructions:

1. Preheat your oven to 350°F (175°C). Grease and flour a 9x13 inch baking dish.
2. In a medium bowl, whisk together the flour, baking powder, and salt. Set aside.
3. In a large mixing bowl, beat the egg yolks and granulated sugar until light and fluffy. Stir in the milk and vanilla extract.
4. Gradually add the flour mixture to the egg yolk mixture, mixing until just combined.
5. In a separate bowl, beat the egg whites until stiff peaks form. Gently fold the beaten egg whites into the batter until fully incorporated.

6. Pour the batter into the prepared baking dish and spread it out evenly. Bake in the preheated oven for 25-30 minutes, or until a toothpick inserted into the center comes out clean.
7. While the cake is baking, prepare the three milks mixture. In a large bowl, combine the sweetened condensed milk, evaporated milk, and whole milk. Mix until well combined.
8. Once the cake is done baking, remove it from the oven and let it cool in the baking dish for 10 minutes.
9. Using a fork or skewer, poke holes all over the surface of the cake.
10. Slowly pour the three milks mixture over the warm cake, making sure to evenly distribute it. Let the cake sit for 30 minutes to allow the liquid to absorb.
11. In the meantime, prepare the topping. In a mixing bowl, beat the heavy cream, powdered sugar, and vanilla extract until stiff peaks form.
12. Spread the whipped cream over the top of the cake. Refrigerate the cake for at least 2 hours, or overnight, to allow the flavors to meld.
13. Before serving, sprinkle ground cinnamon over the top of the cake for garnish, if desired.
14. Slice and serve the Tarta de Tres Leches chilled. Enjoy this deliciously moist and creamy Spanish dessert!

This Tarta de Tres Leches is sure to be a hit at any gathering with its rich and decadent flavor.

Granizado de Limón (Spanish Lemon Granita)

Ingredients:

- 4 cups (960ml) water
- 1 cup (200g) granulated sugar
- Zest of 2 lemons
- 1 cup (240ml) freshly squeezed lemon juice (about 6-8 lemons)

Instructions:

1. In a medium saucepan, combine the water, granulated sugar, and lemon zest. Bring the mixture to a boil over medium heat, stirring occasionally to dissolve the sugar.
2. Once the sugar has dissolved and the mixture comes to a boil, reduce the heat to low and let it simmer for 5 minutes.
3. Remove the saucepan from the heat and let the syrup cool to room temperature.
4. Once the syrup has cooled, strain out the lemon zest and discard it.
5. Stir in the freshly squeezed lemon juice until well combined.
6. Pour the lemon mixture into a shallow baking dish or a metal pan.
7. Place the dish in the freezer and let it freeze for about 1-2 hours, or until the edges start to freeze.
8. Using a fork, scrape the partially frozen edges of the mixture towards the center to break up the ice crystals.
9. Return the dish to the freezer and repeat this process every 30 minutes for about 2-3 hours, or until the entire mixture is frozen and has a granular texture.
10. Once the granita is fully frozen and has a slushy consistency, it's ready to serve.
11. Scoop the granizado de limón into serving glasses or bowls and garnish with a slice of lemon or a sprig of mint, if desired.
12. Serve immediately and enjoy this refreshing Spanish lemon granita on a hot summer day!

Granizado de Limón is a delightful and easy-to-make dessert that's bursting with citrus flavor. It's a perfect palate cleanser or light treat after a meal.

Mantecadas de Astorga (Spanish Sponge Cakes)

Ingredients:

- 1 cup (200g) unsalted butter, at room temperature
- 1 cup (200g) granulated sugar
- 4 large eggs
- 1 teaspoon vanilla extract
- 1 1/2 cups (190g) all-purpose flour
- 1 teaspoon baking powder
- Pinch of salt
- Zest of 1 lemon
- Powdered sugar, for dusting

Instructions:

1. Preheat your oven to 350°F (175°C). Grease and flour a muffin tin or mantecadas molds.
2. In a large mixing bowl, cream together the unsalted butter and granulated sugar until light and fluffy.
3. Add the eggs one at a time, beating well after each addition. Stir in the vanilla extract.
4. In a separate bowl, sift together the all-purpose flour, baking powder, and a pinch of salt.
5. Gradually add the dry ingredients to the wet ingredients, mixing until just combined. Be careful not to overmix.
6. Stir in the lemon zest until evenly distributed throughout the batter.
7. Fill each muffin tin or mantecadas mold about two-thirds full with the batter.
8. Bake in the preheated oven for 15-20 minutes, or until the mantecadas are golden brown and a toothpick inserted into the center comes out clean.
9. Remove the mantecadas from the oven and let them cool in the pan for a few minutes before transferring them to a wire rack to cool completely.
10. Once cooled, dust the mantecadas with powdered sugar before serving.

Mantecadas de Astorga are wonderfully light and fluffy, with a delicate crumb and a hint of lemon flavor. Enjoy these traditional Spanish sponge cakes with a cup of coffee or tea for a delightful snack or dessert!

Pionono (Spanish Rolled Sponge Cake)

Ingredients:

For the Sponge Cake:

- 6 large eggs, at room temperature
- 1/2 cup (100g) granulated sugar
- 1/2 cup (65g) all-purpose flour
- 1 teaspoon vanilla extract
- Pinch of salt

For the Filling:

- 1 cup (about 300g) dulce de leche, cream, or jam

Instructions:

1. Preheat your oven to 350°F (175°C). Grease a 9x13 inch baking sheet and line it with parchment paper, leaving some overhang on the sides for easy removal.
2. In a large mixing bowl, beat the eggs and granulated sugar with an electric mixer on high speed until pale and thick, about 5-7 minutes.
3. Add the vanilla extract and a pinch of salt to the egg mixture and beat for another minute.
4. Sift the all-purpose flour over the egg mixture in small batches, gently folding it in with a spatula until just combined. Be careful not to overmix and deflate the batter.
5. Pour the batter into the prepared baking sheet and spread it out evenly with a spatula.
6. Bake in the preheated oven for 10-12 minutes, or until the cake is lightly golden and springs back when gently pressed with your finger.
7. While the cake is still warm, carefully invert it onto a clean kitchen towel or parchment paper dusted with powdered sugar.
8. Gently peel off the parchment paper from the bottom of the cake.
9. Spread the dulce de leche, cream, or jam evenly over the surface of the cake.

10. Starting from one of the shorter edges, carefully roll up the cake along with the filling, using the towel or parchment paper to help you.
11. Once rolled, transfer the pionono to a serving platter, seam side down.
12. Refrigerate the pionono for at least 1 hour before slicing and serving.
13. Optionally, dust the top of the pionono with powdered sugar before serving.

Pionono is a delightful and versatile dessert that can be enjoyed on its own or served with whipped cream or fresh fruit. It's a perfect sweet treat for any occasion!

Buñuelos de Calabaza (Spanish Pumpkin Fritters)

Ingredients:

- 1 cup (200g) pumpkin puree
- 1 cup (125g) all-purpose flour
- 2 tablespoons granulated sugar
- 1 teaspoon baking powder
- 1/4 teaspoon salt
- 1/2 teaspoon ground cinnamon
- 1/4 teaspoon ground nutmeg
- 1 large egg
- 2 tablespoons milk
- Vegetable oil, for frying
- Powdered sugar, for dusting

Instructions:

1. In a mixing bowl, combine the pumpkin puree, flour, granulated sugar, baking powder, salt, cinnamon, and nutmeg. Mix until well combined.
2. In a separate bowl, beat the egg and milk together.
3. Gradually add the egg mixture to the pumpkin mixture, stirring until a thick batter forms. If the batter is too thick, you can add a little more milk to reach the desired consistency.
4. Heat vegetable oil in a deep frying pan or pot to 350°F (175°C).
5. Once the oil is hot, drop spoonfuls of the pumpkin batter into the hot oil, frying in batches to avoid overcrowding the pan. Use a spoon or ice cream scoop to portion the batter.
6. Fry the buñuelos for 2-3 minutes on each side, or until they are golden brown and crispy.
7. Use a slotted spoon to transfer the cooked buñuelos to a plate lined with paper towels to drain any excess oil.
8. Repeat the frying process with the remaining batter until all the buñuelos are cooked.
9. Once all the buñuelos are cooked and drained, dust them with powdered sugar while they are still warm.
10. Serve the buñuelos de calabaza warm as a delicious snack or dessert.

These Spanish pumpkin fritters are wonderfully crispy on the outside and soft and fluffy on the inside, with a hint of warm spices from the cinnamon and nutmeg. They're perfect for enjoying with a cup of coffee or hot chocolate on a chilly day!

Torrijas de Vino (Wine-Soaked Spanish French Toast)

Ingredients:

For the Torrijas:

- 1 loaf of day-old bread (such as French bread or baguette), sliced into thick slices
- 2 cups (480ml) red wine (such as Rioja or other Spanish red wine)
- 1/2 cup (100g) granulated sugar
- 1 cinnamon stick
- Zest of 1 orange
- Vegetable oil, for frying

For the Garnish:

- Granulated sugar
- Ground cinnamon

Instructions:

1. In a saucepan, combine the red wine, granulated sugar, cinnamon stick, and orange zest. Heat over medium heat, stirring occasionally, until the sugar has dissolved and the mixture comes to a gentle simmer. Let it simmer for 5 minutes to infuse the flavors.
2. Remove the saucepan from the heat and let the wine mixture cool slightly.
3. In the meantime, place the sliced bread in a shallow dish large enough to hold the slices in a single layer.
4. Once the wine mixture has cooled slightly, pour it over the sliced bread, making sure all the bread is soaked. Let the bread soak for about 10-15 minutes, turning the slices halfway through to ensure they soak evenly.
5. Heat vegetable oil in a large frying pan or skillet over medium heat.
6. Once the oil is hot, carefully transfer the soaked bread slices to the pan, shaking off any excess liquid. Fry the torrijas in batches, being careful not to overcrowd the pan, until they are golden brown and crispy on both sides, about 2-3 minutes per side.
7. Once cooked, transfer the torrijas to a plate lined with paper towels to drain any excess oil.

8. While still warm, sprinkle the torrijas generously with granulated sugar and ground cinnamon.
9. Serve the torrijas de vino warm or at room temperature as a delicious and indulgent dessert.

These wine-soaked Spanish French toast torrijas are rich, aromatic, and bursting with flavor. They're a perfect treat to enjoy during special occasions or any time you're craving something sweet and comforting.

Sobaos Pasiegos (Spanish Butter Cakes)

Ingredients:

- 1 cup (225g) unsalted butter, at room temperature
- 1 cup (200g) granulated sugar
- 4 large eggs
- 2 cups (250g) all-purpose flour
- 1 teaspoon baking powder
- 1/4 teaspoon salt
- 1 teaspoon vanilla extract
- Zest of 1 lemon (optional)

Instructions:

1. Preheat your oven to 350°F (175°C). Grease and flour a muffin tin or Sobaos Pasiegos molds if you have them.
2. In a large mixing bowl, cream together the unsalted butter and granulated sugar until light and fluffy.
3. Add the eggs one at a time, beating well after each addition. Stir in the vanilla extract and lemon zest if using.
4. In a separate bowl, sift together the all-purpose flour, baking powder, and salt.
5. Gradually add the dry ingredients to the wet ingredients, mixing until just combined. Be careful not to overmix.
6. Fill each muffin tin or Sobaos Pasiegos mold about two-thirds full with the batter.
7. Bake in the preheated oven for 20-25 minutes, or until the cakes are golden brown and a toothpick inserted into the center comes out clean.
8. Remove the cakes from the oven and let them cool in the pan for a few minutes before transferring them to a wire rack to cool completely.
9. Once cooled, the Sobaos Pasiegos are ready to serve. Enjoy them with a cup of coffee or tea for a delicious treat!

These Sobaos Pasiegos are perfect for breakfast, snack, or dessert. They have a rich buttery flavor with a hint of sweetness, making them a favorite in Spanish cuisine.

Tarta de Chocolate y Almendras (Chocolate Almond Tart)

For the crust:

- 1 1/4 cups (155g) all-purpose flour
- 1/4 cup (30g) almond flour
- 1/4 cup (50g) granulated sugar
- 1/2 cup (115g) unsalted butter, chilled and cut into small cubes
- 1 large egg yolk
- 1-2 tablespoons ice water

For the filling:

- 1 cup (200g) dark chocolate chips or chopped dark chocolate
- 1 cup (240ml) heavy cream
- 1/4 cup (50g) granulated sugar
- 2 large eggs
- 1 teaspoon vanilla extract
- 1/2 cup (50g) sliced almonds, toasted

Instructions:

1. Preheat your oven to 350°F (175°C). Grease a 9-inch tart pan with a removable bottom.
2. In a food processor, combine the all-purpose flour, almond flour, and granulated sugar. Pulse to mix.
3. Add the chilled butter cubes and pulse until the mixture resembles coarse crumbs.
4. Add the egg yolk and 1 tablespoon of ice water. Pulse until the dough comes together. If the dough is too dry, add another tablespoon of ice water.
5. Press the dough into the bottom and up the sides of the prepared tart pan.
6. Place the tart pan in the freezer for 15-20 minutes to chill the crust.
7. Once chilled, bake the crust in the preheated oven for 15-20 minutes, or until lightly golden. Remove from the oven and let it cool slightly.
8. While the crust is cooling, prepare the filling. In a small saucepan, heat the heavy cream over medium heat until it just begins to simmer. Remove from heat.

9. Place the chocolate chips in a heatproof bowl. Pour the hot cream over the chocolate and let it sit for 1-2 minutes.
10. Stir the chocolate and cream together until smooth and well combined. Let the mixture cool slightly.
11. In a separate bowl, whisk together the granulated sugar, eggs, and vanilla extract until well combined.
12. Gradually pour the chocolate mixture into the egg mixture, whisking constantly, until smooth.
13. Pour the chocolate filling into the cooled tart crust.
14. Sprinkle the toasted sliced almonds evenly over the top of the chocolate filling.
15. Bake the tart in the preheated oven for 20-25 minutes, or until the filling is set and the almonds are golden brown.
16. Remove the tart from the oven and let it cool completely before slicing and serving.
17. Serve the chocolate almond tart at room temperature, optionally garnished with whipped cream or a dusting of cocoa powder.

Enjoy your decadent Chocolate Almond Tart!

Goxua (Basque Custard Dessert)

For the Custard:

- 2 cups (480ml) whole milk
- 4 large egg yolks
- 1/2 cup (100g) granulated sugar
- 1/4 cup (30g) cornstarch
- 1 teaspoon vanilla extract
- Zest of 1 lemon (optional)

For the Assembly:

- 8 slices of sponge cake (you can use store-bought or homemade)
- 1/4 cup (60ml) rum or brandy (optional)
- 1 cup (240ml) heavy cream
- 2 tablespoons powdered sugar
- Ground cinnamon, for garnish

Instructions:

1. In a saucepan, heat the whole milk over medium heat until it just begins to simmer. Remove from heat and set aside.
2. In a mixing bowl, whisk together the egg yolks, granulated sugar, and cornstarch until smooth and creamy.
3. Gradually pour the warm milk into the egg yolk mixture, whisking constantly to prevent the eggs from cooking.
4. Once the milk and egg mixture is well combined, pour it back into the saucepan and return it to the stove over medium heat.
5. Cook the custard mixture, stirring constantly, until it thickens and coats the back of a spoon, about 5-7 minutes. Do not let it boil.
6. Remove the custard from the heat and stir in the vanilla extract and lemon zest, if using. Let the custard cool to room temperature.
7. While the custard is cooling, soak the sponge cake slices in rum or brandy if desired.

8. Once the custard has cooled, assemble the Goxua. Place one slice of soaked sponge cake at the bottom of each serving glass or bowl.
9. Spoon a layer of custard over the sponge cake.
10. Repeat with another layer of soaked sponge cake followed by another layer of custard.
11. In a separate bowl, whip the heavy cream and powdered sugar until stiff peaks form.
12. Spoon or pipe a dollop of whipped cream on top of each Goxua.
13. Sprinkle ground cinnamon over the whipped cream for garnish.
14. Refrigerate the Goxua for at least 1 hour before serving to allow the flavors to meld.
15. Serve chilled and enjoy your delicious Basque custard dessert!

Goxua is a delightful combination of creamy custard, sponge cake, and whipped cream, with a hint of rum or brandy for extra flavor. It's a perfect dessert to enjoy on special occasions or any time you're craving something sweet and indulgent.

Brazo de Gitano (Spanish Swiss Roll)

For the Sponge Cake:

- 4 large eggs
- 1/2 cup (100g) granulated sugar
- 1 teaspoon vanilla extract
- 1/2 cup (60g) all-purpose flour
- 2 tablespoons (15g) cornstarch
- 1/2 teaspoon baking powder
- Pinch of salt

For the Filling:

- 1 cup (240ml) heavy cream
- 2 tablespoons powdered sugar
- 1 teaspoon vanilla extract
- Fruit preserves or jam (such as strawberry or apricot), for spreading

Instructions:

1. Preheat your oven to 350°F (175°C). Grease and line a 10x15 inch baking sheet with parchment paper, leaving some overhang on the sides.
2. In a mixing bowl, beat the eggs and granulated sugar with an electric mixer until pale and fluffy, about 5-7 minutes.
3. Beat in the vanilla extract until well combined.
4. In a separate bowl, sift together the all-purpose flour, cornstarch, baking powder, and salt.
5. Gradually fold the dry ingredients into the egg mixture until just combined, being careful not to overmix and deflate the batter.
6. Pour the batter into the prepared baking sheet and spread it out evenly with a spatula.
7. Bake in the preheated oven for 10-12 minutes, or until the cake is golden brown and springs back when gently pressed with your finger.
8. While the cake is baking, place a clean kitchen towel on a flat surface and dust it with powdered sugar.
9. Once the cake is done baking, immediately invert it onto the prepared kitchen towel. Carefully peel off the parchment paper.

10. Starting from one of the shorter edges, carefully roll up the cake along with the kitchen towel. This will help the cake retain its shape when rolled with the filling later.
11. Let the rolled cake cool completely on a wire rack.
12. While the cake is cooling, prepare the filling. In a mixing bowl, whip the heavy cream, powdered sugar, and vanilla extract until stiff peaks form.
13. Once the cake has cooled, carefully unroll it from the kitchen towel.
14. Spread a layer of fruit preserves or jam evenly over the surface of the cake.
15. Spread the whipped cream filling evenly over the fruit preserves or jam.
16. Carefully roll up the cake again, this time without the kitchen towel, starting from the same edge as before.
17. Place the rolled cake seam side down on a serving platter.
18. Slice and serve the Brazo de Gitano chilled, optionally dusting with powdered sugar for garnish.

Enjoy your delicious Spanish Swiss roll filled with whipped cream and fruit preserves or jam!

Piñonate (Spanish Pine Nut Confection)

Ingredients:

- 1 cup (200g) granulated sugar
- 1 cup (240ml) water
- 2 cups (200g) pine nuts
- 1 cup (120g) all-purpose flour
- Zest of 1 lemon
- 1/2 teaspoon ground cinnamon
- Pinch of salt
- Vegetable oil, for greasing

Instructions:

1. Preheat your oven to 350°F (175°C). Grease a 9x9 inch baking dish with vegetable oil and line it with parchment paper, leaving some overhang on the sides for easy removal.
2. In a saucepan, combine the granulated sugar and water. Bring the mixture to a boil over medium heat, stirring occasionally, until the sugar has dissolved.
3. Reduce the heat to low and simmer the sugar syrup for about 5 minutes, or until it thickens slightly.
4. Remove the sugar syrup from the heat and let it cool slightly.
5. In a large mixing bowl, combine the pine nuts, all-purpose flour, lemon zest, ground cinnamon, and a pinch of salt.
6. Gradually pour the cooled sugar syrup over the pine nut mixture, stirring until well combined and the mixture forms a thick dough.
7. Transfer the dough to the prepared baking dish and press it down evenly with a spatula or your hands.
8. Bake in the preheated oven for 25-30 minutes, or until the Piñonate is golden brown and set.
9. Remove the Piñonate from the oven and let it cool completely in the baking dish.
10. Once cooled, use the parchment paper overhang to lift the Piñonate out of the baking dish. Transfer it to a cutting board and slice it into squares or diamonds.
11. Serve the Piñonate at room temperature as a sweet treat or dessert.

Piñonate is a delightful and nutty Spanish confection that's perfect for enjoying with a cup of coffee or tea. It's sweet, crunchy, and packed with flavor from the pine nuts, cinnamon, and lemon zest. Enjoy!

Leche Merengada (Spanish Meringue Milk)

Ingredients:

- 4 cups (960ml) whole milk
- 1 cinnamon stick
- Zest of 1 lemon
- 1/2 cup (100g) granulated sugar
- 4 large egg whites
- Ground cinnamon, for garnish (optional)

Instructions:

1. In a saucepan, combine the whole milk, cinnamon stick, and lemon zest. Heat the mixture over medium heat until it just begins to simmer. Remove from heat and let it steep for about 15-20 minutes to infuse the flavors.
2. After steeping, strain the milk mixture through a fine-mesh sieve to remove the cinnamon stick and lemon zest. Return the infused milk to the saucepan.
3. Add the granulated sugar to the infused milk and heat over medium heat, stirring constantly, until the sugar has dissolved completely. Remove from heat and let the mixture cool to room temperature.
4. In a clean mixing bowl, beat the egg whites with an electric mixer on high speed until stiff peaks form.
5. Gently fold the beaten egg whites into the cooled milk mixture until well combined.
6. Transfer the Leche Merengada to a pitcher or individual glasses and refrigerate until chilled.
7. Before serving, give the Leche Merengada a good stir to incorporate any settled egg whites.
8. Optionally, sprinkle ground cinnamon over the top of each serving for garnish.
9. Serve the Leche Merengada cold and enjoy its refreshing flavor!

Leche Merengada is a delightful drink that's creamy, subtly sweet, and fragrant with cinnamon and lemon. It's perfect for sipping on a warm day or as a light and refreshing dessert after a meal.

Coca de Sant Joan (Spanish Midsummer Cake)

Ingredients:

For the Dough:

- 3 cups (375g) all-purpose flour
- 1/2 cup (100g) granulated sugar
- 1/2 cup (120ml) warm milk
- 1/3 cup (80ml) olive oil
- 2 large eggs
- Zest of 1 lemon
- Zest of 1 orange
- 1 packet (7g) active dry yeast
- Pinch of salt

For the Topping:

- 1/2 cup (75g) pine nuts or candied fruits (such as cherries or orange peel)
- 2 tablespoons granulated sugar

Instructions:

1. In a small bowl, dissolve the yeast in the warm milk and let it sit for about 5-10 minutes, or until frothy.
2. In a large mixing bowl, combine the flour, granulated sugar, pinch of salt, lemon zest, and orange zest.
3. Make a well in the center of the dry ingredients and add the olive oil, eggs, and activated yeast mixture.
4. Mix everything together until a soft dough forms. If the dough is too sticky, you can add a little more flour.
5. Knead the dough on a lightly floured surface for about 5-7 minutes, or until it becomes smooth and elastic.
6. Place the dough in a lightly greased bowl, cover it with a clean kitchen towel or plastic wrap, and let it rise in a warm place for about 1-2 hours, or until doubled in size.

7. Once the dough has risen, preheat your oven to 350°F (175°C).
8. Punch down the dough to release the air and transfer it to a lightly greased baking sheet. Use your hands to shape it into a round or oval shape, about 1/2 inch thick.
9. Arrange the pine nuts or candied fruits on top of the dough and sprinkle with granulated sugar.
10. Bake in the preheated oven for 25-30 minutes, or until the cake is golden brown and cooked through.
11. Remove the Coca de Sant Joan from the oven and let it cool slightly before slicing and serving.
12. Serve the Coca de Sant Joan warm or at room temperature as a delicious treat to celebrate Sant Joan!

Coca de Sant Joan is a wonderful way to celebrate the arrival of summer with its bright citrus flavors and crunchy toppings. Enjoy it with a cup of coffee or tea for a delightful midsummer treat.

Pan de Higos (Spanish Fig Bread)

Ingredients:

- 2 cups (300g) dried figs, stems removed
- 1 cup (150g) almonds, walnuts, or hazelnuts, chopped
- 1/4 cup (60ml) honey
- 1 teaspoon ground cinnamon
- 1/2 teaspoon ground cloves
- Pinch of salt
- Additional chopped nuts or sesame seeds for coating (optional)

Instructions:

1. Place the dried figs in a food processor and pulse until they are finely chopped and form a sticky paste.
2. In a mixing bowl, combine the chopped nuts, honey, ground cinnamon, ground cloves, and a pinch of salt.
3. Add the fig paste to the nut mixture and mix until everything is well combined and forms a thick dough-like consistency.
4. Line a small loaf pan with parchment paper, leaving some overhang on the sides for easy removal.
5. Press the fig mixture firmly into the loaf pan, smoothing the top with a spatula.
6. If desired, sprinkle additional chopped nuts or sesame seeds over the top of the fig mixture and press them lightly into the surface.
7. Cover the pan with plastic wrap and refrigerate for at least 2-3 hours, or until firm.
8. Once firm, remove the Pan de Higos from the loaf pan and transfer it to a cutting board.
9. Use a sharp knife to slice the Pan de Higos into thick slices or bite-sized pieces.
10. Serve the Pan de Higos as a sweet treat or snack. It pairs well with cheese, crackers, or a glass of wine.
11. Store any leftover Pan de Higos in an airtight container in the refrigerator for up to two weeks.

Pan de Higos is a delightful and nutritious snack that's perfect for enjoying any time of day. It's packed with the natural sweetness of figs and the crunch of nuts, making it both satisfying and delicious.

Cuajada (Spanish Curd Cheese Dessert)

Ingredients:

- 4 cups (960ml) whole milk
- 1/4 cup (60ml) water
- 1/4 cup (50g) granulated sugar (adjust to taste)
- 1 cinnamon stick (optional)
- Zest of 1 lemon (optional)
- 2 tablespoons cornstarch (dissolved in 1/4 cup water)

Instructions:

1. In a saucepan, combine the whole milk, water, granulated sugar, cinnamon stick (if using), and lemon zest (if using). Heat the mixture over medium heat until it just begins to simmer.
2. Once the mixture is simmering, remove the cinnamon stick and lemon zest, if using.
3. Gradually add the cornstarch mixture to the simmering milk, whisking constantly to prevent lumps from forming.
4. Continue to cook the mixture, stirring constantly, until it thickens to a custard-like consistency, about 5-7 minutes.
5. Remove the saucepan from the heat and let the Cuajada mixture cool slightly.
6. While still warm, pour the Cuajada mixture into individual serving cups or a large serving dish.
7. Let the Cuajada cool to room temperature, then refrigerate for at least 2-3 hours, or until fully chilled and set.
8. Once chilled, the Cuajada is ready to serve. Optionally, you can sprinkle ground cinnamon on top for garnish before serving.
9. Enjoy the Cuajada as a creamy and refreshing dessert on its own, or drizzle with honey for extra sweetness.

Cuajada is a simple yet delicious dessert that's perfect for serving after a Spanish meal or as a light and refreshing treat on a warm day. Its creamy texture and subtle sweetness make it a favorite among both kids and adults.

Almendrados (Spanish Almond Cookies)

Ingredients:

- 200g almond flour
- 200g powdered sugar
- 2 egg whites
- 1 teaspoon almond extract
- Whole almonds (optional, for decoration)

Instructions:

1. Preheat oven: Preheat your oven to 180°C (350°F) and line a baking sheet with parchment paper.
2. Mix dry ingredients: In a mixing bowl, combine the almond flour and powdered sugar.
3. Whip egg whites: In a separate bowl, whip the egg whites until they form stiff peaks.
4. Combine ingredients: Gently fold the whipped egg whites into the almond flour mixture. Add almond extract and continue folding until well combined. Be careful not to deflate the egg whites too much.
5. Form cookies: Using your hands or a spoon, form small balls of dough and place them on the prepared baking sheet. Flatten each ball slightly with your fingers. If desired, press a whole almond into the center of each cookie for decoration.
6. Bake: Bake the cookies in the preheated oven for about 12-15 minutes, or until they are lightly golden around the edges.
7. Cool: Allow the cookies to cool on the baking sheet for a few minutes, then transfer them to a wire rack to cool completely.
8. Serve: Once cooled, serve and enjoy these delightful almond cookies with a cup of coffee or tea.

Feel free to adjust the sweetness or almond flavor to your liking, and don't hesitate to experiment with different variations, such as adding a sprinkle of cinnamon or a drizzle of chocolate on top. Buena suerte!

Suspiros de Monja (Spanish Nun's Sighs)

Ingredients:

- 4 large eggs
- 150g powdered sugar
- 150g all-purpose flour
- Zest of 1 lemon
- Vegetable oil (for frying)
- Cinnamon sugar (for coating)

Instructions:

1. Separate eggs: Begin by separating the egg yolks from the whites. Place the egg whites in a clean, dry mixing bowl and set aside.
2. Beat egg whites: Using an electric mixer or a whisk, beat the egg whites until they form stiff peaks.
3. Add sugar: Gradually add the powdered sugar to the beaten egg whites, continuing to beat until the mixture is glossy and holds stiff peaks.
4. Fold in flour: Gently fold the all-purpose flour and lemon zest into the beaten egg white mixture until just combined. Be careful not to overmix, as this could deflate the batter.
5. Heat oil: In a deep frying pan or pot, heat vegetable oil to 170°C (340°F) over medium heat.
6. Form the suspiros: Using two spoons or a piping bag, carefully drop small portions of the batter into the hot oil. You can shape them into small balls or elongated shapes resembling "sighs." Fry the suspiros in batches, being careful not to overcrowd the pan.
7. Fry until golden: Fry the suspiros for about 2-3 minutes, or until they are golden brown and crispy on the outside.
8. Drain and coat: Once cooked, remove the suspiros from the oil using a slotted spoon and drain them on paper towels to remove excess oil. While still warm, roll the suspiros in cinnamon sugar until coated evenly.
9. Serve: Serve the Nun's Sighs warm or at room temperature. They are best enjoyed fresh, but you can store any leftovers in an airtight container for a day or two.

These delightful treats are perfect for enjoying with a cup of coffee or tea. Their delicate texture and hint of lemon zest make them a delightful indulgence. ¡Que aproveche!

Sopa de Fresas (Spanish Strawberry Soup)

Ingredients:

- 500g fresh strawberries, hulled and chopped
- 1/4 cup granulated sugar (adjust to taste depending on the sweetness of the strawberries)
- 1/4 cup orange juice
- 1 tablespoon lemon juice
- 1/2 cup cold water
- Fresh mint leaves, for garnish (optional)
- Whipped cream or yogurt, for serving (optional)

Instructions:

1. Prepare the strawberries: Wash the strawberries thoroughly, remove the hulls, and chop them into smaller pieces.
2. Blend the strawberries: In a blender or food processor, puree the strawberries until smooth.
3. Sweeten the soup: Transfer the strawberry puree to a large bowl. Stir in the granulated sugar, adjusting the amount to your taste preference. If the strawberries are very sweet, you may need less sugar.
4. Add citrus juices: Stir in the orange juice and lemon juice to the strawberry mixture. These citrus juices will add brightness and balance to the soup.
5. Thin with water: Gradually add cold water to the strawberry mixture, stirring until you reach your desired consistency. You can add more or less water depending on how thick you want the soup to be.
6. Chill: Cover the bowl with plastic wrap and refrigerate the strawberry soup for at least 1 hour, or until thoroughly chilled.
7. Serve: Ladle the chilled strawberry soup into bowls. Garnish with fresh mint leaves for a pop of color and flavor, if desired. You can also serve the soup with a dollop of whipped cream or yogurt on top for added creaminess.
8. Enjoy: Serve the Spanish Strawberry Soup as a refreshing dessert on its own or as a light finish to a meal. It's perfect for warm weather and showcases the natural sweetness of ripe strawberries.

This delightful soup captures the essence of summer with its vibrant color and fresh strawberry flavor. ¡Buen provecho!

www.ingramcontent.com/pod-product-compliance
Lightning Source LLC
LaVergne TN
LVHW081610060526
838201LV00054B/2183